Docker Easy

The Complete Guide on

Docker World for Beginners

Table of Contents

Chapter 1:
Introduction

1.1 Basic Concept & Terminology:

Let's start by clearing up the concepts and terminology:

1.1.1 Container

Containers are isolated parts of your operating system. They are almost like virtual machines. The difference is that they share a lot of resources, like the kernel, with the host operating system, whereas virtual machines enclose their own operating systems completely. Containers are much lighter to set up and run, but they are just as sufficient for running isolated software. Containers are not exclusive to Docker, and can be used without.

Containers are not a new concept, used since early 30's to the actual patent in 1956 by Malcom McLean. The need of shipping different packages of products with different constraints (size, dimension, weight...) came to the standardization of a shipping model called container. Metaphors aside, in the software production world we find the same needs. And here comes the Software Container, something that bundles the software product and manages its configuration for shipping.

1.1.2 Docker

Docker is a suite of tools for configuring, running and managing containers. The main command line tool, *docker,* can be used to quickly configure and start containers using pre-built images. The suite also includes tools like docker-compose, which is used to quickly start and stop a specific configuration of multiple containers.

Software Container is not a new concept too, but working on it is a hard-low-level job for most of the engineers. Docker, however, turns out being a fast, easy to use, and powerful tool for containerization of your software. Using Docker, you define images which are descriptions of a software environment settings and commands. And from those images, you can run containers which are the actual executable bundle.

Docker is a special kind of virtualization. The advantage over VMWare, Hyper-V, KVM or Xen is that Docker natively uses the kernel of the operating system and has no hypervisor in between. That makes Docker very fast, powerful and performant.

3

1.1.3 Images

Images are pre-built containers for Docker. In virtual machine land they would be comparable to VM snapshots. Anyone can build an image and then share it, and others will be able to run it without having to build it themselves. Also, images can be extended.

1.2 Introduction to Docker

Docker is an open source containerization platform. Docker enables developers to package applications into containers—standardized executable components that combine application source code with all the operating system (OS) libraries and dependencies required to run the code in any environment.

Docker, an open source technology, is used primarily for developing / shipping and running applications. Docker enables you to segregate the applications from your underlying infrastructure so that the software delivery is quicker than ever. Management of infrastructure is made simple and easy via Docker, as it can be managed just the same way how we can manage our own applications. Bringing in the advantages of Docker for shipping, testing, deploying the code – we can significantly reduce the delay between the development stages to hosting the same code on Production.

While developers can create containers without Docker, Docker makes it easier, simpler, and safer to build, deploy, and manage containers. It's essentially a toolkit that enables developers to build, deploy, run, update, and stop containers using simple commands and work-saving automation.

Docker also refers to Docker, Inc., the company that sells the commercial version of Docker, and to the Docker open source project, to which Docker Inc. and many other organizations and individuals contribute.

Your .NET Core container can access a SQL Server database running in a container or a SQL Server instance running on a separate machine. You can even set up a cluster with a mixture of Linux and Windows machines all running Docker, and have Windows containers transparently communicate with Linux containers. Companies big and small are moving to Docker to take advantage of this flexibility and efficiency. The case studies from Docker, Inc. - the company behind the Docker platform - show that you can reduce your hardware requirements by 50% when you move to Docker, while still supporting high availability for your applications. These significant reductions apply equally to on-premises data centers and to the cloud. Efficiency isn't the only gain. When you package your application to run in Docker, you get portability.

You can run your app in a Docker container on your laptop, and it will behave in exactly the same way on a server in your data center and on a virtual machine (VM) in any cloud. This means your deployment process is simple and risk-free because you're deploying the exact same artifacts that you've tested, and you're also free to choose between hardware vendors and cloud providers.

The other big motivator is security. Containers add secure isolation between applications, so you can be confident that if one application is compromised, the attacker can't move on to compromise other apps on the same host. There are wider security benefits in the platform too. Docker can scan the contents of packaged applications and alert you to security vulnerabilities in your application stack. And you can digitally sign packages and configure Docker to run containers only from package authors that you trust. Docker is built from open source components and is shipped as Docker Community Edition (Docker CE) and Docker

Enterprise Edition (Docker EE). Docker CE is free to use and has monthly releases. Docker EE is a paid subscription; it comes with extended features and support and has quarterly releases. Docker CE and Docker EE are available on Windows, and both versions use the same underlying platform, so you can run your apps in containers on Docker CE and EE in the same way.

1.3 Virtualization

Virtualization refers to importing a guest operating system on our host operating system, allowing developers to run multiple OS on different VMs while all of them run on the same host, thereby eliminating the need to provide extra hardware resources. These virtual machines are being used in the industry in many ways as follows:

- Enabling multiple operating systems on the same machine
- Cheaper than the previous methods due to less/compact infrastructure setup
- Easy to recover and do maintenance if there's any failure state
- Faster provisioning of applications and resources required for tasks

- Increase in IT productivity, efficiency, and responsiveness

1.4 Virtualization Host

From the above VM architecture, it is easy to figure out that the three guest operating systems acting as virtual machines are running on a host operating system. In virtualization, the process of manually reconfiguring hardware and firmware and installing a new OS can be entirely automated; all these steps get stored as data in any files of a disk. Virtualization lets us run our applications on fewer physical servers. In virtualization, each application and operating system live in a separate software container called VM. Where VMs are completely isolated, all the computing resources like CPUs, storage, and networking are pooled together, and they are delivered dynamically to each VM by a software called a hypervisor. However, running multiple VMs over the same host leads to degradation in performance. As guest operating systems have their own kernel, libraries, and many dependencies running on a single host OS, it takes up large occupation of resources such as the processor, hard disk and, especially, its RAM. Also, when we use VMs in virtualization, the bootup process takes a long time that would affect efficiency in the case of real-time applications. In order to overcome such limitations, containerization was introduced.

1.5 Containerization

Containerization is a technique in which virtualization takes containerization to the operating system level. In containerization, we virtualize the resources of the operating system. It is more efficient because no guest operating system consumes host resources; instead, the containers only use the host operating system and share the relevant libraries and resources only when necessary. The necessary binaries and container libraries run in the host kernel, which speeds up processing and execution. Simply put, containerization (containers) is a lightweight virtualization technology that acts as an alternative to hypervisor virtualization. Bundle any application in a container and run it without thinking about dependencies, libraries and binary files!

As we were introduced to containerization and virtualization, we know that both allow us to run multiple operating systems on a host machine.

Now, what are the differences between them? Let's check out the below table to understand the differences.

Virtualization	Containerization
Virtualizes hardware resources	Virtualizes only OS resources
Requires the complete OS installation for every VM	Installs the container only on a host OS
A kernel is installed for every virtualized OS	Uses only the kernel of the underlying host OS
Heavyweight	Lightweight
Limited performance	Native performance
Fully isolated	Process-level isolation

In the case of containerization, all containers share the same host operating system. Multiple containers get created for every type of application making them faster but without wasting the resources, unlike virtualization where a kernel is required for every OS and lots of resources from the host OS are utilized.

1.3 Containers vs Virtual Machines

Terms "Containers" and "Virtual Machines" are often used interchangeably, however, this is often a misunderstanding. But both are just different methods to provide Operating System Virtualization.

Standard virtual machines generally include a full Operating System, OS Packages and if required, few applications. This is made possible by a Hypervisor which provides hardware virtualization to the virtual machine. This allows for a single server to run many standalone operating systems as virtual guests.

Containers are similar to virtual machines except that Containers are not full operating systems. Containers generally only include the necessary OS Packages and Applications. They do not generally contain a full operating system or hardware virtualization, that's why these are "lightweight".

1.4 Why use containers?

Containers are made possible by operating system (OS) process isolation and virtualization, which enable multiple application components to share the resources of a single instance of an OS kernel in much the same way that machine virtualization enables multiple virtual machines (VMs) to share the resources of a single hardware server.

Containers offer all the benefits of VMs, including application isolation, cost-effective scalability, and disposability. But the additional layer of abstraction (at the OS level) offers important additional advantages:

- Lighter weight: Unlike VMs, containers don't carry the payload of an entire OS instance—they include only the OS processes and dependencies necessary to execute the code.

- Greater resource efficiency: With containers, you can run several times as many copies of an application on the same hardware as you can using VMs. This can reduce your cloud spending.

- Improved developer productivity: Compared to VMs, containers are faster and easier to deploy, provision, and restart. This makes them ideal for use in continuous integration and continuous delivery (CI/CD) pipelines and a better fit for development teams adopting Agile and DevOps practices.

1.5 Why use Docker?

Docker is so popular today that 'Docker' and 'containers' are used interchangeably, but the first container-related technologies were available for years—even decades—before Docker was released to the public in 2013. Most notably, in 2008, LXC (for Linux Containers) was implemented in the Linux kernel, fully enabling virtualization for a single instance of Linux.

The first versions of Docker leveraged LXC exclusively, but Docker soon developed its own custom containerization technology that enabled the following:

Improved—and seamless—portability: While LXC containers often reference machine-specific configurations, Docker containers run without modification across any desktop, data center, and cloud environment.

Even lighter weight and more granular updates: With LXC, multiple processes can be combined within a single container. With Docker containers, only one process can run in each container. This makes it possible to build an application that can continue running while one of its parts is taken down for an update or repair.

Automated container creation: Docker can automatically build a container based on application source code.

Container versioning: Docker can track versions of a container image, roll back to previous versions, and trace who built a version and how. It can even upload only the deltas between an existing version and a new one.

Container reuse: Existing containers can be used as base images—essentially like templates for building new containers.

Shared container libraries: Developers can access an open-source registry containing thousands of user-contributed containers.

For these reasons, Docker adoption quickly exploded and continues to surge. At this writing, Docker Inc. reports 105 billion container downloads—up from 50 billion just one year ago—and more than 750 enterprise Docker customers.

1.6 Benefits of Docker

Running applications in containers instead of virtual machines is fast gaining momentum in the IT world. The technology is considered to be one of the fastest growing in recent history thanks to it being adopted by key names in the industry alongside many software vendors. At its heart of this ecosystem lies Docker, a platform that allows users to pack, distribute and manage Linux applications within containers. The company and its software have grown immensely since the moment they penetrated the market, now seeking to invest in furthering the usability of the container technology.

1. Fast, consistent delivery of your applications:

Docker enables and also streamlines the development lifecycle into a disciplined environment where developers are allowed to work in these standardized environments with the use of local containers that provide the applications and services. Docker Containers form the biggest usage for the Continuous Integration and Continuous Development workflows (CI / CD).

2. Consider the following example scenario:

Developers can concentrate on coding the modules locally and then it can be shared over to their colleagues using the Docker containers.

The developers can put Docker to use in pushing their applications into a test like an environment and also execute automated and manual regression tests.

Developers if they find bugs, they can put in their efforts in resolving them and then push the fix into the same local environment and then test the fix for correct working as well.

Once the testing phase is completed, delivering the fix to the Customer is nothing difficult as it is just going to be pushing the fix into the Production environment from the Test environment.

3. Responsive deployment and scaling:

Docker with its container-based platform makes it very easy and also allows highly portable workloads. Docker containers have the flexibility running on a developer's laptop, a physical machine, a virtual machine, a virtual machine in a data center, on cloud providers, on-premise providers, or an amalgam of all the mentioned environments until now. Dynamically managing the workloads is very easy with the Docker's portability and light weighted nature. It also makes it every easy to scale up or to tear down applications and services, as and how the business dictates it to.

4. Running more workloads on the same hardware:

As discussed in the above sections that Docker is lightweight, along with it, it is lightning fast as well. It provides viable, cost-effective alternative to its counterparts as like the hypervisor-based virtual machines. This enables than you can consume more on these resources and at the same time achieve the business goals as well. It is very much recommended for high-density environments and also for the small/medium deployments where there is always more to be done with fewer resources.

1.7 Why is Docker so popular

Docker is popular because of the possibilities it opens for software delivery and deployment. Many common problems and inefficiencies are resolved with containers.

The six main reasons for Docker's popularity are:

1. **Ease of use**

   Much of Docker's popularity is its ease of use. Docker can be learned quickly, mainly because of the many resources available to learn how to create and manage containers. Docker is open source, so all you need to get started is a computer with an operating system that supports Virtualbox, Docker for Mac / Windows or that supports containers natively, such as Linux.

2. **Faster scaling of systems**

   Containers allow much more work for much less computer equipment. In the early days of the Internet, the only way to evolve a website was to buy or rent more servers. The cost of popularity was related, in a linear fashion, to the cost of expansion. Popular sites have become the victims of their own success and have spent tens of thousands of dollars on new material. Containers allow data center operators to bundle many more workloads into less hardware. Shared equipment means lower costs. Operators can deposit these profits or transfer the savings to their customers.

3. Better software delivery

Delivery of software using containers can also be more efficient. The containers are portable. They are also completely autonomous. Containers include an isolated disk volume. This volume accompanies the container as it is developed and implemented in various environments. Software dependencies (libraries, runtimes, etc.) are sent with the container. If a container works on your machine, it will work the same way in a development, preparation, and production environment. Containers can eliminate common configuration variation issues by implementing binaries or simple code.

4. Flexibility

The operation of containerized applications is more flexible and resistant than that of containerized applications. Container orchestrators manage the execution and monitoring of hundreds or thousands of containers.

Container orchestrators are very powerful tools for managing large implementations and complex systems. Perhaps the single most popular thing that Docker currently has is Kubernetes, currently the most popular container orchestrator.

5. Software-defined networking

Docker supports software defined networks. Docker CLI and Engine allow operators to define isolated networks for containers, without having to touch a single router. Developers and operators can design systems with complex network topologies and define networks in configuration files. It is also a security benefit. The containers of an application can run in an isolated virtual network, with strictly controlled entry and exit routes.

6. The rise of microservices architecture

The increase in microservices has also contributed to the popularity of Docker. Microservices are simple functions, generally accessible via HTTP / HTTPS, that do one thing and do it well. Software systems generally start out as "monoliths," in which a single binary supports many different system functions. As they grow, monoliths can become difficult to maintain and deploy. Microservices divide a system into simpler functions that can be implemented independently. Containers are excellent hosts for microservices. They are independent, easy to implement and effective.

1.8 The Docker Platform:

Docker provides the flexibility of packaging and running the application in a loosely coupled environment that surpasses the hardware related boundaries called as a Container. The levels of isolation and also the Docker security makes it possible to run many containers at the same time on a host which is Docker enabled. Containers can be thought of as the Virtual Computers but with the only difference of reduced OS. In other words, Containers are light weighted as they do not really need to run on a hypervisor but can run directly on the Host machine's Kernel. This also means that there can be more containers on a given Docker enabled host than if it were to be using Virtual machines. An irony here is that you can run Docker containers within hosts which are virtual machines itself!

Docker provides the required tooling and also a platform to manage the lifecycle of your Docker containers:

- We can develop applications and their supporting components using containers.
- With the above, the container becomes the basic unit for distribution and also in testing application.
- When the application is already, we can deploy your application into a production environment. This can either be done as a container or as an orchestrated service. This works the same whether your production environment is a local data center, a cloud provider, or a hybrid of the two.

Chapter 2:
Docker Tools & Terms

Some of the tools and terminology you'll encounter when using Docker include the following:

2.1 DockerFile

Every Docker container starts with a simple text file containing instructions for how to build the Docker container image. DockerFile automates the process of Docker image creation. It's essentially a list of commands that Docker Engine will run in order to assemble the image.

2.2 Docker images

Docker images contain executable application source code as well as all the tools, libraries, and dependencies that the application code needs to run as a container. When you run the Docker image, it becomes one instance (or multiple instances) of the container.

It's possible to build a Docker image from scratch, but most developers pull them down from common repositories. Multiple Docker images can be created from a single base image, and they'll share the commonalities of their stack.

Docker images are made up of layers, and each layer corresponds to a version of the image. Whenever a developer makes changes to the image, a new top layer is created, and this top layer replaces the previous top layer as the current version of the image. Previous layers are saved for rollbacks or to be re-used in other projects.

Each time a container is created from a Docker image, yet another new layer called the container layer is created. Changes made to the container—such as the addition or deletion of files—are saved to the container layer only and exist only while the container is running. This iterative image-creation process enables increased overall efficiency since multiple live container instances can run from just a single base image, and when they do so, they leverage a common stack.

2.3 Docker containers

Docker containers are the live, running instances of Docker images. While Docker images are read-only files, containers are live, ephemeral, executable content. Users can interact with them, and administrators can adjust their settings and conditions.

The current industry standard is to use virtual machines (VMs) to run software applications. Virtual machines run applications in a guest operating system, which runs on virtual hardware powered by the server's host operating system.

Virtual machines are excellent at providing complete process isolation for applications: there are very few ways in which a problem in the host operating system can affect software running on the guest operating system, and vice versa. But this isolation has a great cost: the computation costs spent in hardware virtualization for an OS invited to use are considerable.

Containers take a different approach: by taking advantage of the low-level mechanics of the host operating system, containers provide most of the isolation of virtual machines at a fraction of the computing power.

Containers provide a logical conditioning mechanism in which applications can be abstracted from the environment in which they actually run. This decoupling allows container-based applications to be implemented easily and consistently, whether the target environment is a private data center, the public cloud, or even a developer's laptop. This gives developers the ability to create predictable environments that are isolated from the rest of the applications and can be run anywhere.

From an operations perspective, in addition to portability containers, more granular control of resources is also achieved, which gives your infrastructure greater efficiency which can translate into better use of your IT resources.

2.4 Docker Hub

Docker Hub is the public repository of Docker images that calls itself the "world's largest library and community for container images." It holds over 100,000 container images sourced from commercial software vendors, open source projects, and individual developers. It includes images that have been produced by Docker, Inc., certified images belonging to the Docker Trusted Registry, and many thousands of other images.

All Docker Hub users can share their images at will. They can also download predefined base images to use as a starting point for any containerization project.

2.5 Docker deployment and orchestration

If you're running only a few containers, it's fairly simple to manage your application within Docker Engine itself. But if your deployment comprises thousands of containers and hundreds of services, it's nearly impossible to manage without the help of these purpose-built tools.

2.6 Docker Compose

If you're building an application out of processes in multiple containers that all reside on the same host, you can use Docker Compose to manage the application's architecture. Docker Compose creates a YAML file that specifies which services are included in the application, and can deploy and run containers with a single command. Using Docker Compose, you can also define persistent volumes for storage, specify base nodes, and document and configure service dependencies.

Docker Compose is a tool that came installed along Docker and is useful on the orchestration of different containers. The point is to let your Composer manage the build and the run all of yours projects. Container orchestration is the next level for managing our services lifecycles. We are able to manage and control numerous things like: Load balancing, Redundancy, Resources allocation, Scale up and down the instances, etc.

2.7 Kubernetes

To monitor and manage container lifecycles in more complex environments, you'll need to turn to a container orchestration tool. While Docker includes its own orchestration tool, called Docker Swarm, most developers choose Kubernetes instead.

Kubernetes is an open source container orchestration platform descended from a project developed for internal use at Google. Kubernetes schedules and automates tasks integral to the management of container-based architectures, including container deployment, updates, service discovery, storage provisioning, load balancing, health monitoring, and more.

Docker Swarm is a very popular container orchestrator, but it isn't the only one. Kubernetes is one alternative that has seen huge growth, with most public clouds now offering a managed Kubernetes service. At the time of writing this book, Kubernetes is a Linux-only orchestrator, with Windows support still in beta. You are likely to hear a lot about Kubernetes on your container journey, so it's worth understanding how it compares to Docker Swarm.

First, the similarities – they are both container orchestrators, which means they are clusters of machines that take care of running containers in production at scale. They both run Docker containers, and you can use the same Docker images with Docker

Swarm and Kubernetes. They are both built on open source projects and conform to the Open Container Initiative (OCI), so there's no concern about vendor lock-in. You can start with Docker Swarm and then move to Kubernetes, and vice versa, without changing your apps.

Now, the differences. Docker Swarm is very simple; you can describe a distributed application to run in containers on swarm in just a few lines of markup. To run the same app on Kubernetes, your application description would be four times as much markup, or even more. Kubernetes has many more abstractions and configuration options than swarm, so there are some things you can do with Kubernetes that you can't do with swarm. The cost of that flexibility is complexity, and the learning curve for Kubernetes is very much steeper than for swarm.

Kubernetes will support Windows soon, but it's not likely to offer full feature compatibility between Linux servers and Windows servers for some time. Until then, it's fine to use Docker Swarm – Docker has hundreds of enterprise customers running their production clusters on Docker Swarm. And if you do find Kubernetes has some extra features that you need, it will be much easier to learn Kubernetes once you have a good understanding of swarm.

2.8 How does the docker work

Docker runs under the host system kernel, the containers contains only user space files and all resources, configuration needed, libs, dependencies and executable commands are defined through images which are light and easily adaptable for different purposes.

Differently from VM's, Docker does not emulate the entire OS on the host machine and that is why is so light compared to VM. The Docker Engine works like a middleware managing the containers process along the host OS. The containers with Docker only load the necessary bins/libs for your App to run.

The goods come are notorious when you start using.

- Resource efficiency: You are able to configure disk space, memory usage, libs and bins to load of your container. Being able to create the lightest and efficient environment for your app.
- Compatible: Compatible with Linux, Windows and MacOS distributions.

- Easy to run and fast: Easy installation, command line tools use and optimizations of the building and run containers.

- Software maintenance: Release new versions changing the containers and guaranteeing the right environment.

- Scalability: Scale your service replicating containers as long as your traffic is heavy and turn some down when it is not so bothered.

- Security: The containers are isolated from the host machine, so it can't access anything outside its own boundaries.

- Reproducibility: The containers are a well-defined environment and you can guarantee the same infrastructure over a set of definitions.

2.9 Docker VS Virtual Machines

Docker works with images and containers. Images can be seen as a kind of template or blueprint. An image itself cannot be started. A container is based on an image. If you want to compare it to object-oriented programming, an image is a class and a container is an instance. A Docker image can be seen as a package: in addition to the required runtime, it includes all libraries, config files and of course the application that is to be started. As already mentioned, a Docker container is a running instance of a Docker image that runs completely isolated on the operating system.

A Docker container therefore holds all the data that was processed or generated by this container (e.g. log files). This means that if the container is deleted, all the data it contains is also deleted. Unless there is a volume mount to the local hard drive, i.e.: a folder within the Docker container is mapped to a folder in the host system, both folders are always the same in content, but more on that later. If a service is under heavy load, another container with the same image can be created and the load can then be shared between these containers.

2.10 Docker Engine

The Docker Engine is a client-server application with the following major components running as the internals of it and they are:

- A server that is long-running which is called as a daemon process (the dockerd command).
- A REST API which specifies interfaces that programs can use to communicate with the daemon and also be able to instruct it on what to do next.

- A command-line interface (CLI) client (the docker command).

The CLI uses the Docker provided REST APIs to control or interact with the Docker daemon through scripting or even the direct Docker CLI commands. Many of the other applications also use the underlying APIs and also uses the CLI interface as well. The daemon manages the part of creating and managing the Docker objects as like the Images, Containers, Networks and also the volumes.

2.11 Differences between Docker Enterprise and Community Edition

Docker is a completely free service if it is used in the community version, while the Enterprise version reserves plans at different prices depending on the operating systems on which it must be run.

The community version is aimed at small businesses, to test operations and begin to understand and discover the world of containers.

If you want to do business and publish applications for which a considerable commitment to security is also necessary, it will be more appropriate to choose the Enterprise edition, which adds technical support (even

24 hours / 7 days), the scanner Docker security (which scans docker window images for vulnerabilities), longer software maintenance and much more.

Chapter 3:
Docker Commands & Architecture

3.1 Docker Commands

- ## Listing Containers

We have already seen, in this Docker tutorial, how to list the running containers using the ps command, but now what we want is to list all the containers, regardless of their state. Well, to do that, all we have to do is add the **-a** option as shown below:

```
docker ps -a
```

Now, we can easily distinguish between which container we want to start with and which one to remove.

- ## Removing Containers

After using a container, we would usually want to remove it rather than having it lying around to consume the disk space.

We can use the rm command to remove a container as shown below:

```
docker rm intellipaat-sql
```

- **Removing Images**

We already know how to list all the locally cached images using the images command. These cached images can occupy a significant amount of space, so in order to free up some space by removing unwanted images, we can use the rmi command as shown below:

```
docker rmi intellipaat-sql
```

Now, we know how to remove cached images, but what about the unwanted and unnamed images that we may end up generating during the debugging cycle of creating a new image? These images are denoted with the name, **<none>**. We can remove them all by using the following command:

```
docker rmi $(docker images -q -f dangling=true)
```

- **Listing Ports**

Knowing which ports are exposed by a container beforehand makes our work a lot easier and faster, e.g., Port 3306 is for accessing a MySQL database and Port 80 is for accessing a web server. Using the port command, as shown below, we can display all the exposed ports:

```
docker port intellipaat-sql
```

• Listing Processes

To display processing in a container, we can use the top command in Docker, which is much similar to the top command in Linux.

```
docker top intellipaat-sql
```

• Executing Commands

To execute commands in a running container, we can use the exec command.

For example, if we want to list the contents of the root of the hard drive, we can use the exec command as shown below:

```
docker exec intellipaat-sql ls /
```

We can gain access to the bash shell if we wish to ssh as root into the container we can use the following command:

```
docker exec -it my-est-mysql bash
```

Note: All communications between Docker clients and Docker daemon are secure since they are already encrypted.

- **Running Containers**

The run command is one of the most complicated commands of all the Docker commands. Using this command, we can perform various tasks like configuring security and managing network settings and system resources such as memory, filesystems, and CPU. We can visit the following link to see and understand how to do all of the above and more using the run command.

3.2 Dockerfile

A Dockerfile contains all the instructions, e.g., the Linux commands to install and configure the software. Dockerfile creation, as we already know, is the primary way of generating a Docker image. When we use the build command to create an image, it can refer to a Dockerfile available on our path or to a URL such as the GitHub repository.

3.3 Instructions

The instructions in a Dockerfile are executed in the same order as they are found in the Dockerfile.

There can also be comments starting with the # character in the Dockerfile.

The following table contains the list of instructions available:

Instruction	Description
FROM	The first instruction in the Dockerfile, it identifies an image to inherit from
MAINTAINER	This instruction provides visibility as well as credit to the author of the image
RUN	This instruction executes a Linux command to install and configure
ENTRYPOINT	The final script or application which is used to bootstrap the container and make it an executable application
CMD	This instruction uses a JSON array to provide default arguments to the ENTRYPOINT
LABEL	This instruction contains the name/value metadata about the image

ENV	This instruction sets the environment variables
COPY	This instruction copies files into the container
ADD	This instruction is basically an alternative to the COPY instruction
WORKDIR	This sets a working directory for RUN, CMD, ENTRYPOINT, COPY, and/or ADD instructions
EXPOSE	The ports on which the container listens
VOLUME	This instruction is to create a mount point
USER	An instruction to run RUN, CMD, and/or ENTRYPOINT instructions

3.4 Docker Machine

Docker machine is a command-line utility that is used to manage one or more local machines (which are usually run in separate VirtualBox instances) or remote machines that are hosted on cloud providers, e.g., Amazon Web Services, Microsoft Azure, etc.

How to create a Local Machine?

Docker Toolbox comes with a default Docker machine named 'default.' This is just to give us a taste of it and to get us started with, but we may need multiple machines later on to segment the different containers that are running. To do that, we can use the following command:

```
docker-machine create –d virtualbox intellipaat
```

This command will create a local machine using a VirtualBox image named 'intellipaat'.

3.5 Listing Machines

If we want to list the machines that we have configured, we can run the following command:

```
docker-machine ls
```

Starting and Stopping Machines

We can start the Docker machine that we have created using the following command:

```
docker-machine start intellipaat
```

Now that the Docker machine has started, we will have to configure the Docker command line with which the

Docker daemon should interact. We can use the following command to do this:

```
docker –machine env intellipaat

eval "$(docker-machine env intellipaat)"
```

Now, to stop a machine, use the following command:

```
docker-machine stop intellipaat
```

3.6 Docker Architecture

Docker uses a client-server architecture. The Docker client includes Docker compilation, Docker extraction, and Docker execution. The client approaches the Docker daemon which helps to create, execute and distribute Docker containers. The Docker client and the Docker daemon can be used on the same system; otherwise, we can connect the Docker client to the remote Docker daemon. The two communicate with each other via the REST API, via UNIX sockets or a network.

The basic architecture in Docker consists of three parts:

- Docker Client
- Docker Host

- Docker Registry
- Docker Client

It is the primary way for many Docker users to interact with Docker. It uses command-line utility or other tools that use Docker API to communicate with the Docker daemon. A Docker client can communicate with more than one Docker daemon.

3.6.1 Docker Host

On the Docker host, we have the Docker daemon and Docker objects such as containers and images. First, let's understand the objects on the Docker host, then we will proceed to the operation of the Docker daemon.

3.6.2 Docker Daemon

The Docker daemon helps you listen to requests from the Docker API and manage Docker objects, such as images, containers, volumes, etc. In case we don't want to create an image, we can simply extract an image from the Docker Hub (which could be built by another user). In case we want to create a running instance of our Docker image, we need to issue a run command that creates a Docker container. A Docker

daemon can communicate with other daemons
to manage Docker services.

3.6.3 Docker Registry

The Docker registry is a Docker image
repository used to create Docker containers.
We can use a local / private registry or the
Docker Center, which is the most popular
social example of a Docker repository.

Chapter 4:
Installation of Docker

Let's get started with the installation and workflow of Docker and implement important Docker commands.

4.1 Installing Docker

For installing Docker on Windows and macOS, the process is quite simple. All we have to do is download and install Docker from https://docs.docker.com/toolbox/ which includes Docker client, Docker machine, Compose (Mac only), Kitematic, and VirtualBox.

On the other hand, in the case of Linux, there are several steps that we need to follow. Let's check out.

To install Docker on the Ubuntu box, first, we need to update its packages. To do so, type the below command on the terminal:

```
sudo apt-get update
```

As we are using this command on sudo, after we hit Enter, it will ask for a password. Provide the password and then follow the steps given further in this Docker tutorial.

Now, we must install its recommended packages. For that, just type the below command:

```
sudo apt-get install linux-image-extra-$(uname -r) lin
ux-image-extra-virtual
```

Now, we have successfully installed the prerequisites for Docker. Press 'y' to continue further

```
sudo apt-get install docker- engine
```

Let's move forward in this docker tutorial and install Docker engine

The Docker installation process is complete now. Use the below command to verify if Docker is installed correctly

```
sudo service docker start
```

You will get an output as start: Job is already running: docker

This means that Docker has been started successfully.

4.2 Running a Container

After the installation of Docker, we should be able to run the containers. If we don't have a container to run, then Docker will download the image in order to build the container from the Docker hub and then will build and run it.

We can run a simple 'hello-world' container to crosscheck if everything is working properly. For that, run the following command:

```
docker run hello-world
```

Output:

```
Hello from Docker!
```

This message shows that installation appears to be working correctly.

4.3 Typical Workflow

Docker's typical local workflow allows users to create images, pull images, publish images, and run containers.

Let's understand this typical local workflow from the diagram below:

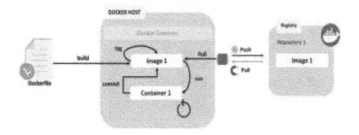

Dockerfile here consists of the configuration and the name of the image pulled from a Docker registry, like a Docker hub. This file basically helps in building an image from it which includes the instructions about container configuration or it can be image pulling from a Docker registry like Docker hub.

Let's understand this process in a little detailed way:

- It basically involves building an image from a Dockerfile that consists of instructions about container configuration or image pulling from a Docker registry, like Docker hub.
- When this image is built in our Docker environment, we should be able to run the image which further creates a container.
- In our container, we can do any operations such as:
  o Stopping the container
  o Starting the container
  o Restarting the container
- These runnable containers can be started, stopped, or restarted just like how we operate a virtual machine or a computer.
- Whatever manual changes are made such as configurations or software installations, these changes in a container can be committed to

making a new image, which can further be used for creating a container from it later.

- At last, when we want to share our image with our team or to the world, we can easily push our image into a Docker registry.

- One can easily pull this image from the Docker registry using the pull command.

4.4 Pulling an Image from the Docker Registry

The easiest way to obtain an image, to build a container from, is to find an already prepared image from Docker's official website.

We can choose from various common software such as MySQL, Node.js, Java, Nginx, or WordPress on the Docker hub as well as from the hundreds of open-source images made by common people across the globe.

For example, if we want to download the image for MySQL, then we can use the pull command:

```
docker pull mysql
```

In case we want the exact version of the image, then we can use:

```
docker pull mysql:5.5.45
```

Output:

```
REPOSITORY    TAG    IMAGE VIRTUAL SIZE<non
e&gt <none> 4b9b8b27fb42 214.4 MB

mysql 5.5.45    0da0b10c6fd8 213.5 MB
```

When we run this command, we can observe the created image with the repository name **<none>**.

Now, to add the identity of the repository, we can use the following command:

```
docker build –t test-intellipaat .
```

After **-t**, we can add any name of our choice to identify our repository.

Output:

```
REPOSITORY TAG IMAGE ID VIRTUAL SIZEtest-inte
llipaat latest 4b9b8b27fb42   214.4 MB

mysql 5.5.45 0da0b10c6fd8   213.5 MB
```

Now, in this Docker tutorial, we shall customize an image manually by installing software or by changing configurations. After completion, we can run the docker commit command to create an image of the running container.

4.5 Running an Image

In order to run a Docker image, all we need to do is use the run command followed by our local image name or the one we retrieved from the Docker hub.

Usually, a Docker image requires some added environment variables, which can be specified with the **-e** option. For long-running processes like daemons, we also need to use the **–d** option.

To start the 'test-intellipaat' image, we need to run the command shown below which configures the MySQL root user's password as documented in the Docker hub MySQL repository's documentation:

```
docker run -e MYSQL_ROOT_PASSWORD=root+1 –d
test-intellipaat
```

To check the container running, use the command below:

```
docker ps
```

This command lists all of our running processes, image, the name they are created from, the command that is run, ports that software are listening on, and the name of the container.

```
CONTAINER ID IMAGE COMMAND30645F307114 te
st-intellipaat "/entrypoint.sh mysql"PORTS NAMES

3306/tcp  shubham_rana
```

We can figure out from the above output that the name of the container is 'shubham_rana' which is an auto-generated one.

When we want to explicitly name the container, the best practice is to use the **–name** option that inserts the name of our choice at container startup:

```
docker run –name intellipaat-sql -e MYSQL_ROOT_P
ASSWORD=root+1 -d est-mysql
```

We can easily name our container with this command.

- **Stopping and Starting Containers**

Once we have our Docker container up and running, we can use it by typing the docker stop command with the container name as shown below:

```
docker stop intellipaat-sql
```

As our entire container is written on a disk, in case we want to run our container again from the state in which we shut it down, we can use the start command:

```
docker start intellipaat-sql
```

Now, let's see how we can tag an image.

- **Tagging an Image**

Once we have our image up and running, we can tag it with a username, image name, and the version number before we push it into the repository using the docker tag command:

```
docker tag intellipaat-sql javajudd/est-mysql:1.0
```

Now, in this Docker tutorial, let's see how we can push an image to the registry.

4.6 Pushing an Image into the Repository

Now, we are ready to push our image into the Docker hub for anyone to use it via a private repository.

- First, go to https://hub.docker.com/ and create a free account
- Next, login to the account using the login command:

```
docker login
```

- Input username, password, and email address we are registered with
- Push our image using the push command, with our username, image, and the version name

Within a few minutes, we will receive a message about our repository stating that our repository has been successfully pushed.

When we go back to our Docker hub account, we will see that there is a new repository as shown below:

4.6 How does Docker work?

Docker as any other counterpart in this arena has a client-server architecture. Docker Daemon which forms the server component can be held responsible for any of the actions that relate with containers. The Docker daemon receives these commands from either the Docker client via the Command Line Interface (CLI) or through the Docker REST APIs. Having said that the Docker client can reside on the same host as that of Docker Daemon or it may be available on a totally different machine altogether.

Images from the basic building blocks in the context of Docker and Containers are built from these images. We can understand Images to be templates with the required configurations of applications and then containers are just copying of these images. Images are always maintained and organized in a layered manner. Each and every change in an image is added as a layer on top of it.

Chapter 5:
Getting Started with
Docker on Windows

5.1 Docker and Windows containers

The user experience for working with Docker is the same, but the way containers are hosted is different. On Windows Server, the process that serves your application actually runs on the server, and there's no layer between the container and the host. In the container, you may see w3wp.exe running to serve a website, but that process is actually running on the server - if you had ten web containers running, you would see ten instances of w3wp.exe in task manager on the server.

Windows 10 doesn't have the same operating system kernel as Windows Server 2016, so in order to provide containers with the Windows Server kernel, Windows 10 runs each container in a very light VM. These are called Hyper-V containers, and if you run a web app in a container on Windows 10, you won't see w3wp.exe running on the host - it's actually running inside a dedicated Windows Server kernel in the Hyper-V container. It's good to understand this distinction. You use the same Docker artifacts and the same Docker commands on Windows 10 and Windows Server 2016, so the processes are the same, but there is a slight performance hit in using Hyper-V containers on Windows 10.

5.2 Windows licensing

On Windows Server, you can also run containers in Hyper-V mode to get increased isolation. This can be useful in multi-tenant scenarios, where you need to expect and mitigate for hostile workloads. Hyper-V containers are separately licensed, but in a high-volume environment, you would use a Datacenter license run Hyper-V containers without individual licenses. Microsoft and Docker, Inc. have partnered to provide Docker EE at no cost with Windows Server 2016. The price of the Windows Server license includes Docker EE Basic, which gives you support to run applications in containers. If you have problems with a container or with the Docker service, you can raise it with Microsoft and they can go on to escalate it to Docker engineers.

5.3 The Docker service and Docker command–line

The Docker CLI is very simple to use; you use commands like docker container run to run an application in a container and docker container rm to remove a container. You can also configure the Docker API to be remotely accessible and configure your Docker CLI to connect to a remote service. This means you can manage a Docker host running in the cloud using Docker commands on your laptop. The setup to allow remote access should also include encryption.

5.4 Docker images

The output is a Docker image. In this case, the image will have a logical size of about 11 GB, but 10 GB of that is the Windows Server Core image you're using as a base, and that image can be shared as the base across many other images. The Docker image is like a snapshot of the filesystem for one version of your application. The image is static, and you distribute it using a registry.

5.5 Image Registries

The most popular registries are the public ones hosted by Docker:

- Docker Hub is the original registry, which has become hugely popular for open source projects in the Linux ecosystem. It has over 600,000 images stored and has hosted over 12 billion image pulls.

- Docker Cloud is where you store images you build yourself, and you can configure images to be public or private. It's suitable for internal products, where you can limit access to the images. You can set up Docker Cloud to automatically build images from Dockerfiles stored in GitHub—currently, this is supported only for Linux-based images, but Windows support is coming soon.

- Docker Store is where you get commercial software, pre-packaged as Docker images. Vendors are increasingly supporting Docker as a platform for their own applications, and you will find software from Microsoft, Oracle, HPE, and more on Docker Store. In a typical workflow, you might build images as part of a CI pipeline and push them to a registry if all the tests pass. The image is then available for other users to run your application in a container.

5.6 Docker Containers

A container is an instance of an application created from an image. The image contains the entire application stack and also specifies the process for starting the application, so Docker knows what to do when running a container. You can run multiple containers from the same image, and you can run containers in different ways. Start your application with the Docker container running, specifying the name of the image and its configuration options. The distribution is integrated with the Docker platform, so if you do not have a copy of the image on the host on which you are trying to run the container, Docker will first extract the image. It then starts the specified process and its application runs in a container. Containers do not need a fixed allocation of CPU or memory, and the processes in their application can use as much host computing power as necessary. You can run dozens of containers on modest hardware, and unless all the applications try to use a large number of CPUs at the same time, they will run simultaneously. You can also start containers with resource limits to limit the amount of CPU and memory to which they have access. Docker provides container runtime, packaging and distribution of images. In a small and developing environment, you will manage individual containers on a single Docker host, which would be your laptop or a test server. When you go into production, you will need high availability and the ability to climb, and that comes with the Docker swarm.

You start your application with docker container run, specifying the name of the image and your configuration options. Distribution is built into the Docker platform, so if you don't have a copy of the image on the host where you're trying to run the container, Docker will pull the image first. Then it starts the specified process, and your app is running in a container. Containers don't need a fixed allocation of CPU or memory, and the processes for your application can use as much of the host's compute power as they need. You can run dozens of containers on modest hardware, and unless the applications all try and use a lot of CPU at the same time, they will happily run concurrently. You can also start containers with resource limits to restrict how much CPU and memory they have access to. Docker provides the container runtime as well as image packaging and distribution. In a small environment and in development, you will manage individual containers on a single Docker host, which would be your laptop or a test server. When you move to production, you'll need high availability and the option to scale, and that comes with Docker swarm.

5.7 Docker Swarm

In swarm mode Docker uses exactly the same artifacts, so you can run your app across 50 containers in a 20-node swarm, and the functionality will be the same as when you run it in a single container on your laptop. On the swarm, your app is more performant and tolerant of failure, and you'll be able to perform automated rolling updates to new versions. Nodes in a swarm use secure encryption for all communication, using trusted certificates for each node. You can store application secrets as encrypted data in the swarm too, so database connection strings and API keys can be saved securely, and the swarm will deliver them only to containers that need them. Docker is an established platform. It's new to Windows Server 2016, but it arrived on Windows after four years of releases on Linux. Docker is written in Go, which is a cross platform language, and only a minority of code is specific to Windows. When you run Docker on Windows, you're running an application platform that has had years of successful production use.

5.8 Docker Security Scanning

A minimal Docker image could still contain software with known vulnerabilities. Docker images use a standard, open format, which means tools can be reliably built to navigate and inspect image layers. One tool is Docker Security Scanning, which examines the software inside Docker images for vulnerabilities.

Docker Security Scanning looks at all the binary files in the image, in your application dependencies, the application framework, and even the operating system. Every binary is checked against multiple Common Vulnerability and Exploit (CVE) databases, looking for known vulnerabilities. If any issues are found, Docker reports the details. Docker Security Scanning is available on Docker Hub for official repositories, on Docker Cloud for your private repositories, and on DTR for your own private registry.

If you find vulnerabilities in your images, you can see exactly where they are and decide how to mitigate them. You could try removing the binaries altogether if you have an automated test suite that you can confidently use to verify that your app still works without them. Or, you may decide that there's no path to the vulnerable code from your application and leave the image as it is. However, you manage it, knowing that there are vulnerabilities in your application stack is extremely useful. Docker Security Scanning can work on each push, so you get immediate feedback if a new version introduces a vulnerability. It can also work on a schedule, so if a new vulnerability is discovered that affects an existing image, you get alerted to that too. This could identify a problem in an old dependency, which you could address by updating package versions in your Dockerfile.

Chapter 6:
Conclusion

6.1 Conclusion

This book is aimed at anyone who wants to learn about the Docker world, whether you're an experienced IT student or developer looking to parlay existing skills into a new environment.

I'd suggest that it's worth doing additional reading around any unfamiliar concept that comes up as you work through this book, as Docker knowledge tends to tie together synergistically; the more you have, the more readily you'll understand new concepts as you expand your toolkit.

Beyond the transfer of knowledge and practical skills, this book looks to achieve a more important goal; specifically, to discuss and convey some of the qualities that are common to skilled Docker practitioners. These include creativity, demonstrated both in the definition of sophisticated architectures and problem- specific cleaning techniques. Rigor is another key quality, emphasized throughout this book by a focus on measuring performance against meaningful targets and critically assessing early efforts.

We have got a detailed understanding of Docker workflow, its need, useful Docker commands, along with Docker images and containers. We hope you have enjoyed learning about "The Complete Guide on Docker World for Beginners". Docker is a continuously developing field. Because of this, there are some considerations to keep in mind as you work with docker methodologies, or analyze the impact of docker processes.

As you finished the book, I wish you the best of luck and encourage you to enjoy yourself as you go, tackling the content prepared for you and applying what you've learned to new domains.

Good Luck!